ROYAL COURT

C000164050

Royal Court Theatre presents

LADYBIRD

by Vassily Sigarev
translated by Sasha Dugdale

First performance at the Royal Court Jerwood Theatre Upstairs
Sloane Square, London on 5 March 2004.

LADYBIRD is presented as part of the International Playwrights Season 2004, a Genesis Project with additional support from the British Council.

LADYBIRD

by **Vassily Sigarev**
translated by Sasha Dugdale

Cast in order of appearance
Lera **Christine Bottomley**
Arkasha **Jason Done**
Slavik **Burn Gorman**
Yulka **Anna Madeley**
Dima **Daniel Mays**
Waster/Old Woman **Kevin McMonagle**

Director **Ramin Gray**
Designer **Lizzie Clachan**
Lighting Designer **Nigel Edwards**
Sound Designer **Ian Dickinson**
Assistant Director **Noah Birksted-Breen**
Casting **Lisa Makin, Amy Ball**
Production Manager **Sue Bird**
Stage Managers **Suzanne Bourke, Nicole Keighley**
Costume Supervisor **Jemimah Tomlinson**
Movement **Sarah Beard**
Company Voice Work **Patsy Rodenburg**
Set Construction by **Simon Renton**

THE COMPANY

Vassily Sigarev (writer)
For the Royal Court: Black Milk, Plasticine.
Other theatre includes: The Vampire's Family, The
Lie Detector, The Russian Lottery.
Awards include: Evening Standard's Charles
Wintour Award 2002 for Most Promising
Playwright, Anti-Booker Prize, Debut Prize
(Plasticine 2000); Eureka Prize (Black Milk 2002).
Vassily has been part of the Russian 'New Writing'
Group which has worked with the Royal Court
since 1999.

Noah Birksted-Breen (assistant director)
For the Royal Court: The Lounge Act (Young
Writers Programme).
As a director, other theatre includes: Hand in Glove
(White Bear); Cyrano de Bergerac (Buskin Drama
Society); Sparkiffs (Burton-Taylor Theatre, Oxford).
As a writer: Outside Inn, Day's Night (Embassy
Theatre); Sparkiffs (Burton-Taylor Theatre, Oxford).
As a translator: The Mad Ones, A Klavier for
Beginners/Shadows, My Little Cherry Orchard (St.
Petersburg Akimov State Theatre, Russia).

Christine Bottomley
Theatre includes: The Pleasureman (Citizens).
Television includes: Early Doors, Heartbeat, Burn It,
Grease Monkeys, The Bill, Dalziel & Pascoe,
EastEnders, Inspector Lynley Mysteries.
Film includes: Mike Leigh Untitled 03.

Lizzie Clachan (designer)
Co-founder of Shunt in 1998 and since then has
worked with the company on all its productions:
Ballad of Bobby Francois, The Tennis Show,
Sightings and Dance Bear Dance.
Other design includes: Royal Exchange Manchester,
Streets Alive, London Bubble, Theatre Venture, The
World Famous, Oxford House and Big Fish
Theatre.

Ian Dickinson (sound designer)
For the Royal Court: Notes on Falling Leaves,
Loyal Women, The Sugar Syndrome, Blood,
Playing the Victim, Fallout, Flesh Wound,
Hitchcock Blonde (& Lyric), Black Milk,
Crazyblackmuthafuckin'self, Caryl Churchill
Shorts, Imprint, Mother Teresa is Dead, Push
Up, Workers Writes, Fucking Games, Herons,
Cutting Through the Carnival.
Other theatre includes: Port (Royal Exchange,
Manchester); Night of the Soul (RSC
Barbican); Eyes of the Kappa (Gate); Crime
and Punishment in Dalston (Arcola Theatre);
Search and Destroy (New End, Hampstead);
Phaedra, Three Sisters, The Shaughraun,
Writer's Cramp (Royal Lyceum, Edinburgh);
The Whore's Dream (RSC Fringe, Edinburgh);
As You Like It, An Experienced Woman Gives
Advice, Present Laughter, The Philadelphia
Story, Wolks World, Poor Superman, Martin
Yesterday, Fast Food, Coyote Ugly, Prizenight
(Royal Exchange, Manchester).
Ian is Head of Sound at the Royal Court.

Jason Done
Theatre includes: States of Shock (BAC);
A Hard Day's Night (Hull Truck).
Television includes: Sea of Souls, Burn It, In
Deep, Murder, Band of Brothers, The King &
I, Where the Heart is, Merlin, The Passion,
Wokenwell, Blood & Peaches, It Must Be
Love, The Andersons.
Film includes: The Barber of Siberia, The
English Patient.

Sasha Dugdale (translator)
Sasha has translated several Russian plays for
the Royal Court, including Black Milk and
Plasticine by Vassily Sigarev; Terrorism and
Playing the Victim by the Presnyakov
Brothers. In 2003 her first collection of poetry
Notebook was published by Carcanet /
Oxford Poets. She won an Eric Gregory
Award for poems from this collection.

Nigel Edwards (lighting designer)
For the Royal Court: Fallout, Bailengaire, Cleansed, 4.48 Psychosis.
Other theatre includes: Bloody Mess, The Voices, Scar Stories, Disco Relax, Sing Me a Song to Unfrighten Me, Dirty Work, Pleasure, Showtime, Speak Bitterness, Hidden J, Club of No Regrets, Emmanuelle Enchanted, Marina and Lee, Some Confusions (Forced Entertainment); Roberto Zucco, Shadows, The Mysteries, Victoria, The Tempest (RSC); Penny Dreadful, Baldy Hopkins, Tie Me Down (The Right Size); Claire de Luz, If We Shadows, Sangre (Insomniac); Sleeping Around, Crave, The Cosmonaut's Last Message, Riddance, Splendour (Paines Plough); Maps for Lost Lovers, Plague On Both Your Houses, (NYT); The Maids (Young Vic); Triumph of Love (Almeida); The Oresteia (RNT); Under The Curse, The Ballad of Yachiyo (Gate); One Minute, Arabian Night, The Boy Who Left Home (ATC); Inconceivable, Mr Heracles (West Yorkshire Playhouse); Dirty Butterfly (Soho); The Misanthrope (Gate, Dublin); Sexual Perversity in Chicago (Comedy).

Burn Gorman
Theatre includes: Tiny Dynamite (Paines Plough/Frantic Assembly); The Green Man (Bush /Plymouth); Ethel & Ernest (Nottingham Playhouse); Destination (Riverside/Volcano); Shooting Stars (Old Red Lion); Morning to Midnight (ENO); Traffic & Weather, Hidden Markings (Contact Theatre); Underbetitled (Royal Exchange Studio); Princess Sharon (Scarlet Theatre); The Herbal Bed (Library Theatre); Christmas Carol (Communicado).
Television includes: The Good Thief, Casualty, Mersey Beat, Coronation Street, The Shoreditch Twat.
Film includes: Colour Me Kubrick, Redlightrunners, Layer Cake, The Bully Boys, Love is Not Enough, Runners, Van Boys.
Burn produces and performs with Hip Hop groups Drool Skool and Decknology, working with artists including Neneh Cherry, Groove Armada and Fatboy Slim and is co-founder of performance group The Fold.

Ramin Gray (director)
For the Royal Court: Advice to Iraqi Women, Terrorism, Night Owls, Just a Bloke, Push Up, How I Ate a Dog.
Other theatre includes: The Child, The Invisible Woman (Gate); Cat and Mouse (Sheep) (Théâtre National de l'Odéon, Paris & Gate); Autumn and Winter (Man in the Moon); A Message for the Broken-Hearted (Liverpool Playhouse & BAC); At Fifty She Discovered the Sea, Harry's Bag, Pig's Ear, A View from the Bridge (Liverpool Playhouse); The Malcontent (Latchmere). Ramin is International Associate at the Royal Court.

Anna Madeley
Theatre includes: The Roman Actor, The Malcontent (RSC & Gielgud, West End); Love in a Wood,
A Russian in the Woods (RSC); Eye Contact (Riverside Studios); Sense & Sensibility (Exeter & tour); Romeo & Juliet (Orange Tree, Richmond); Be My Baby (Soho & Pleasance); The Merry Wives of Windsor (RSC).
Television includes: The Royal, Dinner of Herbs, The Strangerers, Dad, An Unsuitable Job for a Woman: Playing God, Cold Feet.
Film includes: Something for the Weekend, Circular File, Guest House Paradiso, Wonderful World, Back Home.

Daniel Mays
For the Royal Court: The One with the Oven, Just a Bloke.
Television includes: EastEnders, In Deep, Manchild, Dead Casual, NCS, Bodily Harm, Tipping the Velvet, Keen Eddie.
Film includes: Pearl Harbour, All or Nothing, Rehab, Mike Leigh Untitled 2003.

Kevin McMonagle
For the Royal Court: Ambulance, Karate Billy Comes Home, Thyestes.
Other theatre includes: The Prime of Miss Jean Brodie, Hamlet, Woyzeck (Royal Lyceum, Edinburgh); Broken Glass, Hamlet (West Yorkshire Playhouse); Further Than the Furthest Thing, The Changeling, The Resistable Rise of Arturo Ui, Black Snow (RNT); Richard III (RSC); A Message for the Broken-Hearted (Liverpool Playhouse/ BAC); Wishbones, Heart Throb (Bush); The Miser (Akasaki Playbox, Tokyo); Cat & Mouse (Sheep) (Théâtre National de l'Odéon, Paris); Macbeth, Muir, Salvation, Clyde Nouveau (Tron); The Plough and The Stars (Citizens); Brighton Rock, Les Liaisons Dangereuses (Coventry); The Hypochondriac, Electra, Orestes (Leicester Haymarket).

THE ENGLISH STAGE COMPANY AT THE ROYAL COURT

The English Stage Company at the Royal Court opened in 1956 as a subsidised theatre producing new British plays, international plays and some classical revivals.

The first artistic director George Devine aimed to create a writers' theatre, 'a place where the dramatist is acknowledged as the fundamental creative force in the theatre and where the play is more important than the actors, the director, the designer'. The urgent need was to find a contemporary style in which the play, the acting, direction and design are all combined. He believed that 'the battle will be a long one to continue to create the right conditions for writers to work in'.

Devine aimed to discover 'hard-hitting, uncompromising writers whose plays are stimulating, provocative and exciting'. The Royal Court production of John Osborne's Look Back in Anger in May 1956 is now seen as the decisive starting point of modern British drama and the policy created a new generation of British playwrights. The first wave included John Osborne, Arnold Wesker, John Arden, Ann Jellicoe, N F Simpson and Edward Bond. Early seasons included new international plays by Bertolt Brecht, Eugène Ionesco, Samuel Beckett, Jean-Paul Sartre and Marguerite Duras.

The theatre started with the 400-seat proscenium arch Theatre Downstairs, and then in 1969 opened a second theatre, the 60-seat studio Theatre Upstairs. Some productions transfer to the West End, such as Terry Johnson's Hitchcock Blonde, Caryl Churchill's Far Away, Conor McPherson's The Weir, Kevin Elyot's Mouth to Mouth and My Night With Reg. The Royal Court also co-produces plays which have transferred to the West End or toured internationally, such as Sebastian Barry's The Steward of Christendom and Mark Ravenhill's Shopping and Fucking (with Out of Joint), Martin McDonagh's The Beauty Queen Of Leenane (with Druid Theatre Company), Ayub Khan Din's East is East (with Tamasha Theatre Company, and now a feature film).

Since 1994 the Royal Court's artistic policy has again been vigorously directed to finding and producing a new generation of playwrights. The writers include Joe Penhall, Rebecca Prichard, Michael Wynne, Nick Grosso, Judy Upton, Meredith Oakes, Sarah Kane, Anthony Neilson, Judith Johnson, James Stock, Jez Butterworth, Marina Carr, Phyllis Nagy, Simon Block, Martin McDonagh, Mark Ravenhill, Ayub Khan Din, Tamantha Hammerschlag, Jess Walters, Ché Walker, Conor McPherson,

Simon Stephens, Richard Bean, Roy Williams, Gary Mitchell, Mick Mahoney, Rebecca Gilman, Christopher Shinn, Kia Corthron, David Gieselmann, Marius von Mayenburg, David Eldridge, Leo Butler, Zinnie Harris, Grae Cleugh, Roland Schimmelpfennig, DeObia Oparei, Vassily Sigarev, the Presnyakov Brothers and Lucy Prebble. This expanded programme of new plays has been made possible through the support of A.S.K Theater Projects and the Skirball Foundation, the Jerwood Charitable Foundation, the American Friends of the Royal Court Theatre and many in association with the Royal National Theatre Studio.

INTERNATIONAL PLAYWRIGHTS

Since 1992 the Royal Court Theatre has placed a renewed emphasis on the development of international work and a creative dialogue now exists with theatre practitioners all over the world including Brazil, Cuba, France, Germany, India, Palestine, Russia, Spain, and Uganda. All of these development projects are supported by the British Council and the Genesis Foundation.

The Royal Court has worked with new Russian playwrights since 1999, with over a dozen initiatives including exchanges, seminars and workshops in Moscow, Novosibirsk and Ykaterinburg in collaboration with the British Council and the Genesis Foundation. Exchange events at the Royal Court include Moscow Open City (2000), Evgeny Grishkovets' How I Ate A Dog (2000), New Plays from Russia (2001), Theatre Lozhe The Coalfield and Babii Soldiers' Letters (Steps to Siberia 2002), Ilya Falkovsky's Fishing and the Presnyakov Brothers' We Shall Overcome (International Playwrights 2002). Recent Royal Court productions of new Russian plays include Vassily Sigarev's Plasticine (2002, winner of the Evening Standard's Charles Wintour Award for Most Promising Playwright 2002) and Black Milk (2003), as well as the Presnyakov Brothers' Terrorism (2003) and Playing the Victim (2003, with Told by an Idiot).

International Playwrights Season is produced by the Royal Court International Department: Associate Director **Elyse Dodgson** International Administrator **Ushi Bagga** International Associate **Ramin Gray**

AWARDS FOR
THE ROYAL COURT

The Royal Court was the overall winner of the 1995 Prudential Award for the Arts for creativity, excellence, innovation and accessibility. The Royal Court Theatre Upstairs won the 1995 Peter Brook Empty Space Award for innovation and excellence in theatre.

Michael Wynne won the 1996 Meyer-Whitworth Award for The Knocky. Martin McDonagh won the 1996 George Devine Award, the 1996 Writers' Guild Best Fringe Play Award, the 1996 Critics' Circle Award and the 1996 Evening Standard Award for Most Promising Playwright for The Beauty Queen of Leenane. Marina Carr won the 19th Susan Smith Blackburn Prize (1996/7) for Portia Coughlan. Conor McPherson won the 1997 George Devine Award, the 1997 Critics' Circle Award and the 1997 Evening Standard Award for Most Promising Playwright for The Weir. Ayub Khan-Din won the 1997 Writers' Guild Awards for Best West End Play and Writers' Guild New Writer of the Year and the 1996 John Whiting Award for East is East (co-production with Tamasha).

At the 1998 Tony Awards, Martin McDonagh's The Beauty Queen of Leenane (co-production with Druid Theatre Company) won four awards including Garry Hynes for Best Director and was nominated for a further two. Eugene Ionesco's The Chairs (co-production with Theatre de Complicite) was nominated for six Tony awards. David Hare won the 1998 Time Out Live Award for Outstanding Achievement and six awards in New York including the Drama League, Drama Desk and New York Critics Circle Award for Via Dolorosa. Sarah Kane won the 1998 Arts Foundation Fellowship in Playwriting. Rebecca Prichard won the 1998 Critics' Circle Award for Most Promising Playwright for Yard Gal (co-production with Clean Break).

Conor McPherson won the 1999 Olivier Award for Best New Play for The Weir. The Royal Court won the 1999 ITI Award for Excellence in International Theatre. Sarah Kane's Cleansed was judged Best Foreign Language Play in 1999 by Theater Heute in Germany. Gary Mitchell won the 1999 Pearson Best Play Award for Trust. Rebecca Gilman was joint winner of the 1999 George Devine Award and won the 1999 Evening Standard Award for Most Promising Playwright for The Glory of Living.

In 1999, the Royal Court won the European theatre prize New Theatrical Realities, presented at Taormina Arte in Sicily, for its efforts in recent years in discovering and producing the work of young British dramatists.

Roy Williams and Gary Mitchell were joint winners of the George Devine Award 2000 for Most Promising Playwright for Lift Off and The Force of Change respectively. At the Barclays Theatre Awards 2000 presented by the TMA, Richard Wilson won the Best Director Award for David Gieselmann's Mr Kolpert and Jeremy Herbert won the Best Designer Award for Sarah Kane's 4.48 Psychosis. Gary Mitchell won the Evening Standard's Charles Wintour Award 2000 for Most Promising Playwright for The Force of Change. Stephen Jeffreys' I Just Stopped by to See The Man won an AT&T: On Stage Award 2000.

David Eldridge's Under the Blue Sky won the Time Out Live Award 2001 for Best New Play in the West End. Leo Butler won the George Devine Award 2001 for Most Promising Playwright for Redundant. Roy Williams won the Evening Standard's Charles Wintour Award 2001 for Most Promising Playwright for Clubland. Grae Cleugh won the 2001 Olivier Award for Most Promising Playwright for Fucking Games. Richard Bean was joint winner of the George Devine Award 2002 for Most Promising Playwright for Under the Whaleback. Caryl Churchill won the 2002 Evening Standard Award for Best New Play for A Number. Vassily Sigarev won the 2002 Evening Standard Charles Wintour Award for Most Promising Playwright for Plasticine. Ian MacNeil won the 2002 Evening Standard Award for Best Design for A Number and Plasticine. Peter Gill won the 2002 Critics' Circle Award for Best New Play for The York Realist (English Touring Theatre). Ché Walker won the 2003 George Devine Award for Most Promising Playwright for Flesh Wound. Lucy Prebble won the 2003 Critics' Circle Award for Most Promising Playwright for The Sugar Syndrome.

ROYAL COURT BOOKSHOP

The bookshop offers a wide range of playtexts and theatre books, with over 1,000 titles. Located in the downstairs Bar and Food area, the bookshop is open Monday to Saturday, afternoons and evenings.

Many Royal Court playtexts are available for just £2 including works by Harold Pinter, Caryl Churchill, Rebecca Gilman, Martin Crimp, Sarah Kane, Conor McPherson, Ayub Khan Din, Timberlake Wertenbaker and Roy Williams.

For information on titles and special events, Email: bookshop@royalcourttheatre.com
Tel: 020 7565 5024

PROGRAMME SUPPORTERS

The Royal Court (English Stage Company Ltd) receives its principal funding from Arts Council England, London. It is also supported financially by a wide range of private companies and public bodies and earns the remainder of its income from the box office and its own trading activities. The Royal Borough of Kensington & Chelsea gives an annual grant to the Royal Court Young Writers' Programme.
The Genesis Foundation supports the International Season and Young Writers Festival.

The Jerwood Charitable Foundation supports new plays by new playwrights through the Jerwood New Playwrights series. The Skirball Foundation fund a Playwrights' Programme at the theatre. The Artistic Director's Chair is supported by a lead grant from The Peter Jay Sharp Foundation, contributing to the activities of the Artistic Director's office. Bloomberg Mondays, the Royal Court's reduced price ticket scheme, is supported by Bloomberg. Over the past seven years the BBC has supported the Gerald Chapman Fund for directors.

ROYAL COURT
DEVELOPMENT BOARD
Tamara Ingram (Chair)
Jonathan Cameron
(Vice Chair)
Timothy Burrill
Anthony Burton
Jonathan Caplan QC
Sindy Caplan
Mark Crowdy
Joseph Fiennes
Joyce Hytner
Dan Klein
Gavin Neath
Michael Potter
Ben Rauch
Kadee Robbins
Mark Robinson
William Russell
Sue Stapely
James L Tanner
Will Turner

TRUSTS AND FOUNDATIONS
American Friends of the Royal Court Theatre
Gerald Chapman Fund
Cowley Charitable Trust
The Dorset Foundation
The Foundation for Sport and the Arts
The Foyle Foundation
Francis Finlay Foundation
Genesis Foundation
The Haberdashers' Company
Jerwood Charitable Foundation
The Boris Karloff Charitable Foundation
John Lyon's Charity
The Magowan Family Foundation
The Moose Foundation for the Arts
The Diana Parker Charitable Trust
The Laura Pels Foundation
Quercus Charitable Trust
The Peter Jay Sharp Foundation
Skirball Foundation

SPONSORS
American Airlines
Arts & Business New Partners
Barclays
BBC
Bloomberg
Peter Jones
Royal College of Psychiatrists

BUSINESS MEMBERS
Aviva plc
Burberry
Lazard
Pemberton Greenish
Redwood
Simons Muirhead & Burton
Slaughter and May

MEDIA MEMBERS
Beatwax
Bloomsbury
Buena Vista International (UK) Ltd
Columbia Tristar Films (UK)
Hat Trick Productions
Miramax Films
XL Video UK

PRODUCTION SYNDICATE
Anonymous
Jonathan & Sindy Caplan
Kay Hartenstein Saatchi
Richard & Susan Hayden
Peter & Edna Goldstein
Jack & Linda Keenan
Kadee Robbins
The Viscount & Viscountess Rothermere
William & Hilary Russell
Jan & Michael Topham

INDIVIDUAL MEMBERS
Patrons
Anonymous
Katie Bradford
Ms Kay Ellen Consolver
Mrs Philip Donald
Celeste Fenichel
Tom & Simone Fenton
Jack & Linda Keenan
Richard & Robin Landsberger
Duncan Matthews QC
Ian & Carol Sellars
Jan & Michael Topham
Richard Wilson OBE

Benefactors
Anonymous
Martha Allfrey
Marcus J Burton
Lucy Bryn Davies
Jeremy Conway & Nicola van Gelder
Robyn Durie
Winstone & Jean Fletcher
Joachim Fleury
Homevale Ltd.
Tamara Ingram
Peter & Maria Kellner
Barbara Minto
Nigel Seale
Jenny Sheridan
Brian D Smith
Amanda Vail
Sir Robert & Lady Wilson

Associates
Anonymous
Anastasia Alexander
Brian Boylan
Mr & Mrs M Bungey
Ossi & Paul Burger
Mrs Helena Butler
Lady Cazalet
Carole & Neville Conrad
David & Susan Coppard
Margaret Cowper
Barry Cox
Andrew Cryer
Linda & Ronald F. Daitz
David Day
Zoë Dominic
Kim Dunn
Charlotte & Nick Fraser
Jacqueline & Jonathan Gestetner
Vivien Goodwin
Judy & Frank Grace
Don & Sue Guiney
P. Hobbs - LTRC
Mrs Ellen Josefowitz
David Kaskel & Christopher Teano
Mr & Mrs Tarek Kassem
Carole A. Leng
Lady Lever
Colette & Peter Levy
Mr Watcyn Lewis
David Marks
Nicola McFarland
Rod & Mina McManigal
Eva Monley

Gavin & Ann Neath
Georgia Oetker
Mr & Mrs Michael Orr
Lyndy Payne
Pauline Pinder
William Plapinger & Cassie Murray
William Poeton CBE & Barbara Poeton
Jan & Michael Potter
Jeremy Priestley
Beverley Rider
Lois Sieff OBE
Sue Stapely
Will Turner
Anthony Wigram

THE AMERICAN FRIENDS OF THE ROYAL COURT THEATRE

AFRCT support the mission of the Royal Court and are primarily focused on raising funds to enable the theatre to produce new work by emerging American writers. Since this not-for-profit organisation was founded in 1997, AFRCT has contributed to ten productions. They have also supported the participation of young artists in the Royal Court's acclaimed International Residency.

If you would like to support the ongoing work of the Royal Court, please contact the Development Department on 020 7565 5050.

Arts Council England

Association of **London** Government

ROYAL COURT
SLOANE SQUARE

INTERNATIONAL PLAYWRIGHTS SEASON 2004

A Genesis Project

RUSSIA
Rehearsed Readings
18 & 25 March, 6pm

STATES OF CHANGE
New work from around the world
10 — 13 March

STATES OF VIOLENCE
Rehearsed Readings
10 — 12 March, 7.30pm

THE STATE OF PALESTINE
Seminar **12 March, 2-5pm**

CITY STATES
Rehearsed Readings
13 March, 7.30pm

CUBA REAL
New plays from Cuba
Rehearsed Readings
30 March — 3 April, 7.45pm

CUBAN EVENTS
including music and dance

For more information contact the Box Office.

BOX OFFICE
020 7565 5000
www.royalcourttheatre.com

FOR THE ROYAL COURT

LADYBIRD

Vassily Sigarev

Translated by Sasha Dugdale

Characters

DIMA, *aged nineteen*

SLAVIK, *aged twenty-two*

LERA, *aged twenty*

YUL'KA, *her cousin, aged eighteen*

THE WASTER, *Dima's father, aged fifty*

AN OLD WOMAN

ARKASHA

In the beginning there was nothing. Then man came and built The Town. Houses appeared, streets, squares, shops, schools, factories, public gardens. At first the roads were paved, then tarmacked, with decorated white borders for the public holidays. People appeared on the streets and on the benches, began sneezing at the floating white seeds from the poplar trees; selling sunflower seeds at the factory gates; falling in love. People were born, and they died.

And a Cemetery appeared on the edge of The Town. And people brought their dead there and placed them in holes and sprinkled earth into the holes. They went there on memorial days and for anniversaries and left biscuits and sweets with white fillings. They weeded out the grass with their hands and replaced it with pansies. And the Cemetery began to grow . . .

But people didn't just die. They were born too and so the Town grew as well.

And then at some point the Town and the Cemetery met. People built a five-storey block right next to the Cemetery and began to live in it. To begin with everyone found it horrible, they were afraid to look out of the window. But then they got used to it. They even built metal garages along the Cemetery fence and kept their cars in them and motorbikes and old bits and pieces. They even thought up a name for their block, an amusing one. They called it 'Dead and Alive'. And that's what it's called even now.

And they buried the new dead in a different place.

And it almost seemed as if they'd forgotten about the old dead. They stopped putting out biscuits and sweets with white fillings. They stopped planting pansies. There was nothing there. It became overgrown with grass, extraordinarily long and rampant grass. And the Cemetery was buried in this grass. It disappeared. It ceased to exist. It died. And together with the Cemetery, all of the dead died. For a second time. This time for good . . .

ACT ONE

A brick-built block on the edge of town. It has four storeys and three entrances. Lights shine from the windows and the blinds are visible. The panes of glass are broken and have been taped together. You can see people in the windows. They come over to the windows and glance out. They look out as if they had been waiting for something for a long time and can't wait anymore. They stand there, look out and then turn away. Back into the flats.

And outside the wind is chasing the dead leaves on the roads. It is late autumn. The leaves are falling, landing in puddles. They soak through, then freeze. And the wind laughs and slams the doors to the entrance halls; now it throws itself onto the slate roof, now it knocks quietly at the windows and roars with laughter. And then suddenly it slips into the entrance hall and begins to wail. It wails in a wild and terrible way as if it had seen something strange. Back there . . .

And two GIRLS *follow the wind into the same entrance hall. They stop in front of a door. Look at each other, laugh. They start climbing the stairs. Going up there.*

On every second landing there is a lit bulb in a wire cage. Dry leaves lie on the steps like suspicious bits of paper. The GIRLS *climb slowly, rustling the leaves under their feet, talking about something and laughing in low voices. One of them keeps spitting.*

At last they reach the fourth floor. They stop in front of a door padded with fake leather. They look at each other again and laugh quietly. They ring the doorbell.

A MAN with a shaved head opens the door. He is wearing jeans with nothing on top. He starts smiling.

FIRST GIRL. Hey! He's had a shave! Quick work.

MAN. Did it myself. Keep the fleas off.

FIRST GIRL. Let's have a feel. (*Strokes him on the head.*) Right little hedgehog you are Dima. (*She laughs.*) Fancy a laugh, Yul'ka?

YUL'KA *touches his shaved head.*

Lovely, eh? Like a cactus.

DIMA. Got long, Lera?

LERA. I've got some stuff to do and that . . . haven't got long. I'll be off in a minute.

DIMA. Got yourself a fancy man?

LERA. And you can piss off with your 'fancy man'. Are we coming in? I'll tell you everything in a minute. Wait till you hear. It's a complete fucking mess, that's what it is. Nothing to touch it.

DIMA. That's enough. Come on in then.

YUL'KA *starts taking off her shoes.*

(*Stopping her.*) Leave it, eh.

LERA. What's she up to? (*Looks at the other girl.*) What you doing? Are you mad? It's a pigsty in there. They haven't cleaned the floor in seven years.

DIMA. Don't lie. Six-and-a-half.

LERA. Eight. (*She spits and goes into the room.*)

DIMA. No-one lives that long.

The flat has two rooms. In one room there is a mattress on the ground and piles of books tied with string. There are lots of books, heaps of them, all around the room. A MAN *sleeps on the mattress in the half-darkness, covered by a blanket. In the other room there is exactly the same mattress with crumpled newspaper-coloured sheets on it, two armchairs and a table. A tall,* SKINNY MAN *sits in one of the chairs with his legs stretched out. He is digging out the varnish from the arm of the chair with his fingernail. In the corner of the room there is a pile of stainless steel grave-markers, lying one on top of each other. There are four of them and it is clear that they are not new. Some of them even have little round photographs on them and plaques with dates. The bases of the grave-markers have earth stuck to them. The earth is black as if still damp. The door to the balcony is open. A rubber insulation strip nailed to the balcony door-post sways in the draft. There are no blinds at the windows. The* SKINNY MAN *succeeds in digging out a piece of varnish and puts it in his mouth. He bites it, trying it for taste.*

LERA (*noticing the man in the armchair*). Hey, it's Slavik! Seven foot in his bare feet. You here already?

SLAVIK *smiles. He chews on the piece of varnish.*

Scored, have you?

SLAVIK *continues to smile and shakes his head.*

You shooting up in here?

SLAVIK *shakes his head and smiles.*

Well you're in your bloody element. Talk about . . . what it's called . . . not giving anything away. (*She laughs.*)

DIMA. Slav, stop eating the bloody furniture, eh? It's driving me mad.

LERA. Oh, go on, let him eat, Dima. Look at him – he's all skin and bones!

DIMA. Stop it, Slav, eh. Go and eat the waster's books if you're hungry. He won't mind.

SLAVIK *makes a show of chewing the piece of varnish.* YUL'KA *looks at him and smiles.*

LERA. It's like this, see. This is my cousin. Yul'ka, her name is. I brought her with me. For the company and that. So you bastards don't get bored. So if there's anything from anyone, then there'll be trouble, and I fucking well mean trouble. I'm warning you. She's at college. So I don't even want any filthy language. And no scratching your balls in front of her? Alright?

SLAVIK *grins.*

That goes for you up there, too.

DIMA (*to* YUL'KA). So you're Yulia, then? I'm Dima . . . (*He kisses her hand.*)

LERA. I've warned you, Dim.

DIMA. I'm just introducing myself, alright.

LERA. That's enough. Keep away from her.

YUL'KA. Oh, come on. It's alright. I wasn't born yesterday. We'll sort it out ourselves.

LERA. You know best. Your look-out then. (*Sits down in the armchair and lights a cigarette.*) Anyway, I was telling you . . . You'll wet yourselves when you hear this. The things that's been going on . . .

DIMA. Hang on. Slavik. Let Yul'ka sit down. (*Pause.*) Move it, Slav, eh.

SLAVIK (*stretching, with a groaning voice*). Can't move . . .

LERA. Hey – the big man's got a voice. How's it going, Slavik? How's things?

SLAVIK. Shit. Pure shit.

LERA. Scored, eh?

SLAVIK. Nah. I'm strung out.

LERA. Well go get some.

SLAVIK. No money.

LERA. Just you wait, Slavik, listen to what I've got to say, eh – it'll do your head in.

DIMA. Slav, get your arse out of there. The lady's waiting for you.

YUL'KA. I'll stand. It's OK.

DIMA. Slav. I mean it. You're pissing me off.

SLAVIK. Just a second . . . (*He slides off the chair onto the ground and slumps against the wall. He groans.*)

LERA *laughs.*

DIMA. Have a seat, Yul.

YUL'KA *sits down.* DIMA *crouches beside her and says something to* YUL'KA.

LERA. Come on, you lot. Listen to this.

DIMA. Well go on then.

LERA. So anyway, there I was meeting Yul'ka from the bus and that. We were on our way back and I decided to have a look in the letterbox for some reason. Never looked before and all of a sudden I decided to. And guess what . . . ? Bloody heck! Did my head in, I tell you. Almost died right there on the spot. Yul'ka here saw. See, there was a letter in there. All brightly coloured and that. And my name on the envelope, printed out. Not by hand, but printed. Like in the magazines. And inside it said . . . I can hardly bloody get it out. (*She laughs and rubs her face with her hand.*) Anyway there's this company, called Euroshop, right . . . and it's twelve thousand . . . And all for me . . . dollars, that is . . . I've won them!

DIMA. You're having us on.

LERA. I told you. Ask Yul'ka here.

YUL'KA *nods.*

Anyway, it's a real, serious company. I've got my own registration number and all. The works, in fact. There was three prizes. The first was a car and that. Twenty-five thousand that was. Then came mine. Gold, see. Twelve thousand. But I can take it in cash. I'll have it in cash, course. 'Cause who wants to get stuck with gold. Eh? And then there was a kitchen. Seven-and-a-half thousand. Rubbish, that one. Hardly anything. So now, see, I need a thousand. I have to order something from them, like, become a customer and that. Then they have the right to give me the prize. I've been round to almost everyone's today. No-one will lend me anything. Lend us a thousand roubles, Dim.

DIMA. Where am I going to get it from?

LERA. I'll give you two thousand back.

DIMA. I haven't got it.

LERA. What about the waster?

DIMA. Where would he get it from?

SLAVIK. That's all crap.

LERA. What?

SLAVIK. These prizes and that. I know all about this shit. It's designed for brainless bastards – brainless and aimless.

LERA. Cock off, eh.

SLAVIK. It's a con. You'll see.

LERA. I'll see what? I'll see the money, that's fucking what! I'm getting out of here. And you'll be left. Get it?

SLAVIK. Let's bet on it.

LERA. Yeah, fine. Just cock off, that's all. It's a real, serious firm. With an office at the main post office in Moscow. And a coloured envelope with pictures on it. And then there was a woman, a peasant, a farmworker, holding a pile of money in the picture – she was the last winner, see? And she's definitely not an actress, you can see that. A peasant through and through. In one of those cheapie Chinese cotton housecoats. From the market. See, I know they do it for the advertising. They give out some prizes and the ones that have won them tell others and that's how they get their customers. This money's nothing to them. Loose change.

SLAVIK. Bet you. It's a con.

LERA. Piss off . . . They've got an office at the . . .

SLAVIK. Bet you.

LERA. That's it. You've fucking well ruined my mood. I'm not listening to a word you say. Cock off, right. Lend us a thousand, Dima.

DIMA. I haven't got it. I haven't even got enough for fags tomorrow. I wanted to take a few packs with me at least . . .

SLAVIK. You'll get some there.

DIMA. Come off it. They couldn't care less.

SLAVIK. They have to. Are you supposed to join up just like that, for nothing?

LERA. So where's the party then? Where are the kebabs and that? Balloons and streamers? Who's the one going off to the army? Me?

DIMA. Arkasha'll be here any minute now. He's bringing the stuff with him. I told him I wanted the money in booze and that. I've got about five hundred's worth here. Maybe more. I've already weighed it.

LERA. So why did you invite everyone this early then?

DIMA. He should have been here ages ago. What's the time?

LERA. High time. Dunno. Haven't got a watch.

YUL'KA. After nine.

DIMA. Well, he'll be here soon.

SLAVIK. Did you tell Arkash to bring any gear?

DIMA. Where's he going to get it?

SLAVIK. From a dealer.

DIMA. Oh come off it. How's he going to know where to get it?

SLAVIK. Well, he can bring the money then. And I'll get some from Gela.

DIMA. He's bringing drink and food for the whole amount. We've already agreed. And that's it.

SLAVIK. You cunning bastard. I need a hit. Right now. I'm dying.

DIMA. Have a drink and you'll be fine.

SLAVIK. Thanks a lot. I want something stronger.

DIMA. Well, I want things too, but I don't go on about it all the time.

SLAVIK. Shit . . . Hey! An ant. (*He catches the ant.*) Anyone for an ant? . . . No? Then I will. (*He licks up the ant, shudders and winces.*) Lovely! I've got a whole flat of them myself. The bastards came up from the cemetery. Fuck all left to eat down there. After the

sweets all went, the ants made their way up here.
When I'm really bad, I catch them and eat them. It
makes it a bit better. They've got acid in them of some
sort, haven't they?

YUL'KA. Formic.

SLAVIK. There you go. Reckon you can cook that up?

YUL'KA. What?

LERA. That's enough Slav. Do your muppet thing
instead.

YUL'KA. What thing?

LERA. Muppet. Watch this. Go on, Slav.

*SLAVIK starts silently laughing and waving his head
around in all directions. LERA roars with laughter.
YUL'KA smiles.*

That's from the Muppet Show. Remember it? That
green one, what's his name . . . Kermit. All green and
that. Frog, wasn't he. He used to do that. And there
was another one. With a big nose. Gorilla . . . (*She
looks at* YUL'KA. YUL'KA *shrugs.*) Well, with a big
nose. Looked like one of them Caucasus blokes. Big
lump of a thing. What's his name? (*She clicks her
fingers.*)

Pause.

DIMA. Gonzo.

LERA. Gonzo, thassit! Remember?

YUL'KA shakes her head.

Oh, come on . . . When we were kids. Those puppet
things. You must remember! Like, a cartoon. Eh?

YUL'KA shrugs.

Pause.

SLAVIK. I could do with another ant. (*He gets down on all fours and crawls around the floor looking for one.*)

YUL'KA (*whispering*). Is he . . . a bit . . . up here . . . (*She touches her temple with her finger.*)

LERA. He's a headcase. Friend of Dima's. He's out of it. Talking a load of shit, he was – all that 'brainless and aimless' stuff. Pokes his nose in where he's not wanted. Moron, he is.

DIMA (*jumps up and goes towards the balcony*). Shit. I've still got to get the photos off. Or Arkasha will go ballistic again. (*He gets a screwdriver from the balcony, picks the top grave-marker up from the pile and starts unscrewing the photograph.*)

YUL'KA (*goes over to him and looks*). What's all this?

DIMA. Grave-markers.

YUL'KA. No, honestly.

DIMA. Memorial plaques.

YUL'KA. Do you make them or something?

DIMA. You having a laugh?

YUL'KA. Where are they from then?

DIMA. Over there.

YUL'KA. The balcony?

DIMA. Come here. (*He takes her by the hand and leads her out onto the balcony.*) Can you see?

YUL'KA. What?

DIMA. Over there. On the other side of the street. Behind the garages. Can you see?

YUL'KA. What is it?

DIMA. A goldmine. Or used to be, at any rate.

YUL'KA. What, seriously?

DIMA. A cemetery.

YUL'KA. You mean a real one?

DIMA. No, a toy one. 'Course, a real one. Come on, it's cold out here.

YUL'KA. In a minute. (*She looks.*) Oh yeah, I can see it. You're right. It's a cemetery. How awful. How can you live here? I'd have gone mad long ago.

DIMA. It's fine. This block, d'you know what it's called?

YUL'KA. What?

DIMA. 'Dead and Alive.' Funny, isn't it? Over here the alive, over there the dead. Or the other way round. I'm not sure anymore.

YUL'KA. Nightmare.

LERA. That's enough – you sweethearts are taking your time. Come on in.

DIMA. Let's go.

They go back into the room.

LERA. Dim, I warned you to stay away from her.

DIMA. I was showing her the cemetery.

LERA. And did you show her?

DIMA. Yes.

LERA. Happy now?

YUL'KA. Come on, it's fine, Lera.

LERA. No, it's not 'fine, Lera'. They fuck you, and your mum will be round causing blue murder. I'm responsible for you.

DIMA. Right. That's it. End of film. Credits roll. Want a laugh? Look. (*He runs the screwdriver along the radiator.*) Shhh.

Pause. Everyone listens.

VOICE (*quiet at first, but then growing louder*). Kolya . . . Kolya . . . Kolya . . . Turn on the light, Kolya. It's dark, Kolya. I don't feel well, Kolya. Turn me over, Kolya. My back hurts. It's burning me, Kolya, like a fire. Kolya. Turn me over. Kolya . . . It's the pain, Kolya . . . I don't feel well . . . Kolya . . . Kolya . . .

YUL'KA. What's that?

DIMA. Reality radio.

LERA *laughs.*

YUL'KA. No, seriously.

DIMA. Old lady in the flat downstairs. She's bedridden. Doesn't get up at all.

YUL'KA. And who's Kolya?

DIMA. Her son. Pisshead, like the waster here. He starts drinking and she lies there, shouting all night. Stops me sleeping. I once gave him such a beating in the entrance hall, that I scared myself. Got really mad for some reason. I got hold of him and started having a go at him. Like 'you bastard, why don't you look after your mum, you fucker. She gave birth to you, brought you up and that . . . ' and he just stands there, grinning. So I'm shaking all over with anger and he's out of it, grinning away. Gave him such a punch in the head it brought him straight down. Then I kicked him for about fifteen minutes. That was it. He just lay there. Slavik here dragged me away, thank God. Or I'd have fucking finished him.

SLAVIK. She's got loads of money.

DIMA. Come off it.

SLAVIK. She gets a pension.

DIMA. He drunk his way through that long ago.

SLAVIK. No way. She hides her money from him. I heard him once, trying to get some off her for a bottle. She wasn't having any of it.

DIMA. She hasn't got anything.

SLAVIK. Fancy a bet?

DIMA. Piss off, eh. You're annoying me.

LERA. So where's this Arkasha then, Dima?

DIMA. Just a minute. He'll be here soon. Let me just get these photos off in peace, eh? I've got to get the inscriptions off too. You're all getting in my way. Arkasha will be here in a minute and I haven't got anything ready. He'll kick up a right stink then. He doesn't like taking them with the inscriptions on in case he gets caught by the police. He's a coward. Right. I've got to get on with this. (*He starts unscrewing the photos.*)

SLAVIK. Hey! Another ant! Come here, my lovely . . . (*He catches it and eats it.*)

YUL'KA. So this is all from the cemetery, is it?

LERA. Have you only just got it?

YUL'KA. What, seriously?

LERA (*suddenly shouts*). Dim, be a mate – lend me a thousand!

DIMA (*shouts back*). You be a mate – I haven't got it!

LERA. Dimka . . .

DIMA. What?

LERA. Come here.

DIMA. What? (*He goes over.*)

LERA. Get lost, Yul. (*She gives* DIMA *a hug.*) Dim, my
very bestest neighbour in the whole wide world . . .
(*She whispers something in his ear.*)

YUL'KA *goes out onto the balcony.*

DIMA. I said, I haven't got it.

LERA. The whole lot, Dim. All the add-ons. You've got a
whole two years without women ahead . . .

DIMA (*walking away*). And you've got two years
without men.

LERA. Come here, eh. You have got it. The number of
fucking gravestones you got rid of last week . . . I
know.

DIMA. I haven't got it. When Arkasha comes you can
borrow it off him.

LERA. Will he give it to me?

DIMA. Will you give it to him?

LERA. Cock off. I'm serious. I'll give him two thousand
back. Only I've got to order something. It's urgent.
Like tomorrow. I've got to get out of here. My mum's
driving me mad. She gets drunk and then she sells all
my stuff. And she brought this bloke back recently. In
glasses. She says to me . . . (*Shouts towards the
balcony.*) Put your hands over your ears, Yul'ka! She
says, 'Lera, why don't you go with him. Sleep with
him.' I mean, sleep with him! Go with him! The bitch!
She's a fucking nightmare. She is so out of order.
I just kept quiet, that's all. Went into my room and
he's already lying there. Naked. Wanking. The bastard.
And grinning. So you see Dim, I've got to get out of
here. Right away. And this is my chance. Maybe there

is a God after all. Giving to the ones who need. 'Cause usually it's the ones who have everything that get more. And then more. So there is a God after all.

DIMA. There isn't.

LERA. Cock off.

DIMA. There isn't a God.

LERA. Cock off. There is.

SLAVIK. There is.

LERA. See? So cock off.

SLAVIK. A bloke who lives in the second entrance hall. He's got a dog and it had puppies. He drowned them all and left this one. A little bitch. He's called her God. (*He roars with laughter.*)

DIMA *laughs.*

LERA. I'm just going to fucking well leave you all to it. I can't let myself be led into sin with all you lot here, can I, or he'll turn away from me again. And then everything will go pear-shaped. See?

DIMA. There's no God.

LERA. There is.

DIMA (*looking at the ceiling*). Hey God! Where are you? Come, girl. Sit! Lie down! Over here, God! God! God!

SLAVIK *bursts into laughter.* DIMA *bangs the radiator.*

VOICE. Kolya . . . Kolya!! Kolyaaaa!!

DIMA. God! Kill! Kill! Kill, girl!

YUL'KA *comes in from the balcony.*

LERA (*jumps up, runs over to DIMA and hits him*). Shut it! You wanker! Bastard! Shut the fuck up!

DIMA. What's wrong?

LERA. What's wrong? Come on, Yul'ka, we're getting out of here. Bastards, the lot of them. Pricks. Come on, Yul'ka!

DIMA. Oh come on, Lera. Don't go on.

LERA. You can cock off . . . I've had enough . . . They're bastards. They've really got to me. I want to get out of here . . . away from this bloody cemetery . . . buy myself a flat, a pick-up truck . . . open a shop . . . I'll get some money . . . have kids! Eight of them . . . To get back at the lot of you! I'll find myself a nice husband in a suit . . . with a moustache and . . . just to get back at you! See if I don't! You just wait! (*She sits down in the armchair and cries.*) And she tells me to go with him . . . sleep with him . . . her own daughter . . . her own daughter . . . to go with him . . .

YUL'KA. Ler . . .

LERA. Go with him! Say something like that to your own daughter . . . your own daughter . . .

YUL'KA. Ler . . .

LERA. . . . . Go with him! She can fucking go with him, the cunt . . . I hate her . . . I hate her . . . (*She cries.*)

THE WASTER *comes in from the next room. He stops and stares at them. Smiles. He's drunk.*

THE WASTER. Hallo, lads. Having fun? Pour us a drink.

YUL'KA. Hallo.

DIMA. Eh. Waster. Calm her down, will you? Lend her a thousand.

LERA (*wiping away her tears*). Lend us some, eh, waster? And I'll give you two back later. I need to make an order, urgently. It's a once-in-a-lifetime chance. I can buy myself a flat, a car and a shop all at once. It's a company in Moscow, they've got a head office at the main post office –

SLAVIK. And give us a hundred, you waster.

LERA. Cock off. I got there first. See, there was this old peasant woman. She got a prize too. What do you say, eh, waster?

THE WASTER. What?

LERA. Lend us a thousand.

THE WASTER. I'm, like they say . . . as skint as the day is long . . .

LERA. So why d'you come rushing in then?

THE WASTER. Well, you know. Got a son going into the army, haven't I. Wanted to wish him well. Pour us a drink.

LERA. There isn't anything. Nothing to wish him well with.

THE WASTER. Well, why didn't you say so? Noooo. I'm not one of those . . . I get my drinks elsewhere. I just take a stroll around town and get what I need. I know some real old drinkers, thank God . . . Some do spirits, some schnapps . . . eau de cologne too, by the way . . . I never turn it down . . . I'll let you into a secret: it's a very clean product. Just add water and it turns as white as milk, and they give milk to babies, don't they . . . So I wouldn't come to you for my drink . . . No, I'm here as a father . . . to see you on your way. So anyway, Dimka. My advice is to serve honestly . . . without getting into trouble . . . without any . . . you know what I'm saying . . . Maybe they'll give you a commission. And then you'll be made, and not a useless shit like me. That's it, then. Are you sure you're not hiding anything from me?

DIMA. Nothing.

THE WASTER. Oh come on. A day like this and no booze. Get it out, go on. I can see it hidden under the table. I've got sharp eyes, you know.

DIMA. There's nothing there.

THE WASTER. I can see it sticking out.

DIMA (*angrily*). I said there's nothing!

THE WASTER. Fine. I'll be quiet. It distresses me, upsets me, but that's fine. Alright then, Dim, my boy, I've seen you off and now it's time for me to set off on the long road. The time has come. The cocks are crowing!

DIMA. Off you go then.

THE WASTER. Hang on. I'm not finished yet. Is there really nothing?

DIMA. Nothing.

THE WASTER. Well, here's a poem to send you on your way. One of Esenin's . . . 'We are all departing slowly for that place of blessed peace . . . perhaps my time will come to collect my earthly goods . . . (*Suddenly loud and emphatic.*) Sweet birchwoods!'

DIMA. Stop shouting, you waster.

THE WASTER. 'You, earth! And you, sandy plains!'

SLAVIK *bursts into laughter.*

DIMA. Fuck off, waster.

THE WASTER (*going back and half-whispering*). 'Before these departing crowds I cannot hide my pain.' (*He cries.*) 'In this world I loved too much all that which binds the soul in flesh . . . ' (*He lies down, covers himself with the blanket and is no longer audible.*)

DIMA. Fucking half-wit . . . He used to be something
   big in local education . . . ran the schools and that. But
   when my mum died he went to drink and they threw
   him out. We got a new flat down here. When I was
   younger all the teachers used to tiptoe round me, all
   polite and that . . . By the end I was barely allowed to
   finish. I should give him a beating to remember me by.
   I'm not coming back here whatever. Waster! Come
   and say goodbye!

LERA. Let him be, Dima.

DIMA. No I fucking won't. He ruined my life with all
   his shit so bad that I'll suffer for the rest of mine.
   Waster! Come back here, you bastard! I'm going to
   beat the shit out of you! (*He laughs.*) In your face . . .
   A fucking kicking . . .

SLAVIK. Go for it, Dim! Give him a hiding!

DIMA. Waster! (*He goes into the other room. The others
   follow him.*) Waster! (*He lifts* THE WASTER *from the
   mattress and holds him by the throat.*) Waster, your
   time has come! You'll wish you were dead, bastard!
   What did you do with my happy childhood? Drunk
   your way through it! My rosy childhood! Why didn't I
   take sweets to school like all the other kids on my
   birthday?! You drunk your way through them, bastard!

THE WASTER. I don't . . .

DIMA. Well I do! (*He hits* THE WASTER *across the
   face with his hand.*)

LERA. Stop it, Dima!

DIMA. I'm not stopping now! 'Cause of this bastard I
   pissed myself in junior school. Sat in the back row and
   pissed myself, because I was too scared to ask to go to
   the toilet. When he worked in the schools everyone
   was scared of him. And then when he started drinking

they all took it out on me. Bitches . . . And I sat there and pissed myself and stank like a toilet . . . Right, waster, you'd be better off dead . . . you bastard . . . (*He starts strangling him.*)

YUL'KA. Dima, don't . . .

DIMA *stops. He lets* THE WASTER *go.*

Let's go and have a smoke on the balcony instead.

DIMA. What?

LERA. You've been invited out onto the balcony. Yul'ka, just you don't go complaining afterwards.

YUL'KA. Come on, let's have a smoke.

DIMA. Alright.

They go out onto the balcony. YUL'KA *holds* DIMA *under the arm.* THE WASTER *lies back down and looks at* LERA *with a frightened face.* LERA *kicks him gently and goes out.*

SLAVIK. Hey! An ant! Stop right there, ant! (*He catches it and licks it up.*) Fancy one, Lera?

LERA. Lend us a thousand instead, Slav.

SLAVIK. Why not two while you're at it?

LERA. Well, let's have a fag then instead.

SLAVIK. I've only got the roll-ups . . . Roll-overs . . . (*He roars with laughter.*)

LERA. Cock off with your roll-overs . . . (*She goes into the toilet.*)

SLAVIK *sits on the floor holding an ant on the palm of his hand and playing with it. His face is filled with glee.*

YUL'KA. So why didn't you get out of it? It's easy now. We've got this bloke at college. Had, anyway. They threw him out. So he got out of it, or whatever you do, straight away. Didn't go into the army, anyway. Why didn't you do that?

DIMA. What for?

YUL'KA. What you going to do there?

DIMA. What would I do here?

YUL'KA. I don't know, but life is back here, isn't it? You can go to clubs and that.

DIMA. You can . . .

YUL'KA. You can do what you like.

DIMA. You can . . .

YUL'KA. Well, no point in talking about it. Bit late now. If you like I'll write letters to you. I love writing letters. Would you like that?

DIMA. I don't know where I'll be yet.

YUL'KA. I'll give you my address then and you can write to me first and then I'll write to you.

DIMA. Alright.

YUL'KA. Are those grave-markers really from the cemetery then?

DIMA. Mmm.

YUL'KA. And what do you do with them?

DIMA. Sell them.

YUL'KA. For how much?

DIMA. Ten roubles a kilo.

YUL'KA. And are there a lot there?

DIMA. Used to be. There's a factory here processes stainless steel. As soon as they started buying them we were made – we were loaded. Slavik went and got himself a habit 'cause he had nothing better to do. Then they put policemen round to guard it and they started nicking them themselves. There was total chaos. Then they took the police away and it all started up again. They're almost gone now.

YUL'KA. Come and study at college when they let you out of the army. I'll help you. My dad's dean at a college.

DIMA. I never finished school.

YUL'KA. Well, do evening classes then.

DIMA. I'm as thick as they come.

YUL'KA. No, you're not.

DIMA. I am.

YUL'KA. You're alright. Able.

DIMA (*laughs*). What?

YUL'KA. Able.

DIMA (*laughing*). Able? Well, lucky me.

YUL'KA. Nothing to laugh about. You're an able bloke. I can see that. Slavik there is thick, but you're able.

DIMA. And I'm thick, too.

YUL'KA. No, you aren't. Stop arguing.

DIMA. Alright then. I'll come and study round there then.

YUL'KA. Bet you won't.

DIMA. I will.

YUL'KA. You won't.

DIMA. I will, you'll see.

YUL'KA. You won't.

DIMA. Let's bet on it.

YUL'KA. Alright.

> *She stretches out her hand.* DIMA *takes it and then covers it with his.*

What'll we bet on?

> DIMA *doesn't answer. He stands there silent. A pause.* YUL'KA *smiles.* LERA *runs in.*

LERA. Dima! Have you lost it?

DIMA (*letting go of* YUL'KA*'s hand*). What?

> YUL'KA *goes back into the flat.*

LERA. You and your fucking lovey-dovey . . . her mum will kill me!

DIMA. What was I doing then?

LERA. Touching her up.

DIMA. I wasn't touching her up.

LERA. She's not for you.

DIMA. Who's she for then?

LERA. Whoever. She's still a virgin. No touching, get it?

DIMA. Why you telling me, eh? Was I planning to or something?

LERA. That's it. Cock off! (*Goes back into the room.*) And you an' all, Yul'ka. I mean, not like I didn't warn you.

YUL'KA. We were just having a bet.

LERA. Yeah, right. I know how he bets.

SLAVIK. What you so mad about?

LERA. Nothing. I mean, what did I say when I got here? I told you she wasn't . . . wasn't for any of your tricks. She's a little girl still, isn't she. And Dima here was just getting his paws on her.

DIMA. No, I wasn't.

LERA. Not like I don't know you, eh.

A ring at the door.

DIMA. Right. Shush everyone. That's Arkasha. (*He goes to open the door.*)

LERA. Dima, what should I tell him then?

DIMA. Tell him you need money? I dunno . . .

LERA. D'you reckon he'll give me any?

DIMA. How should I know? Depends how you ask.

LERA. Fuck, Dima . . . (*She gets a pocket mirror out of her bag and tidies herself up.*)

DIMA *opens the door.* ARKASHA *enters. He holds a plastic bag with food and drink in it.*

DIMA. Alright.

ARKASHA. Jesus, Dima, am I your fucking waiter or something? Running round the shops like a blue-arsed fly. Is this home delivery now, eh? Here. (*He pushes the plastic bag at* DIMA.)

DIMA. It's just I'm going into the army and that . . . This was a sort of farewell party.

ARKASHA. Really? Well, good on you. What can I say? Where's the metal?

DIMA. Over there.

ARKASHA. Oh, I see you've got female company. Hello, ladies.

LERA. Hiya.

YUL'KA. Hallo.

SLAVIK. Alright, Arkan.

ARKASHA. And Slava's here. How's things with him? Happy to be alive?

SLAVIK. Shit.

ARKASHA. Oh come on. Bad day, eh?

SLAVIK. I'm comatose.

ARKASHA. Comatose – that's not an overdose. It'll pass. Dim, there's some scales in the bag. Pass them here.

DIMA *gets some bathroom scales out of the bag.*

YUL'KA. Hey, can I weigh myself?

ARKASHA. No.

YUL'KA. Oh. Why not?

ARKASHA. Dima, come on, load them up and we'll check them.

DIMA *puts the plaques on the weighing scales.* ARKASHA *gets out a calculator and taps on it.*

Well, Dim, you're in the shit.

DIMA. What?

ARKASHA. You owe me twenty.

DIMA. How come? I weighed them.

ARKASHA. I don't care whether you weighed them or not. I've got my own scales.

DIMA. Oh fuck. I took the photos off, didn't I. Forgot about that.

ARKASHA. Right. So hand over the twenty.

DIMA. Shit, Arkash, I haven't got it right now. Things are a bit tight at the moment. I haven't even got the money to buy fags for tomorrow. Slavik, give us a twenty.

SLAVIK. Where am I going to it from?

DIMA. Shit, Arkash. What are we going to do?

ARKASHA. Head for the hills . . . Alright. I'll let it pass.

DIMA. You can take the inscriptions if you like. I've got a whole bag. The alloy's much better.

ARKASHA. No, the traders'll kill me if I take those inscriptions. I said I'd let it pass. End of story. Alright, take the stuff out to the car.

DIMA. OK. Right. (*He picks up two grave-markers and carries them out.*)

ARKASHA (*nodding in the direction of the cemetery*). Dim, is it all finished up there?

DIMA. Yeah. That's it. Nothing left.

ARKASHA. Not good. Alright. Go on.

DIMA *goes out.* ARKASHA *looks at* YUL'KA *and smiles.*

Go and weigh yourself then.

YUL'KA. Don't want to.

ARKASHA. What's that in aid of?

YUL'KA. Just don't want to. Changed my mind.

LERA. Can I then?

ARKASHA. Go ahead.

LERA *gets on the scales.*

SLAVIK. Arkan, I've got something urgent to say.

ARKASHA. What's that then, Slav? Money is it?

SLAVIK. Just a hundred, Arkan. Till tomorrow.

LERA. Cock off, Slav. I was first in line.

ARKASHA. And what happens tomorrow? Last pension payment?

SLAVIK. I've got this one grave-marker. Weighs about fifteen kilos. I'll give it to you tomorrow.

ARKASHA. Why tomorrow? Bring it round now.

SLAVIK. Everyone's asleep round at mine. I'll do it tomorrow. I'm on my last legs here. Comatose. I'll do it tomorrow.

ARKASHA. Are you taking the piss? I'm not going to drive all the way to yours for one grave-marker tomorrow. Bring it round.

SLAVIK. Arkasha, for fuck's sake, I'll do it tomorrow.

ARKASHA. Forget it.

SLAVIK. Alright, fuck it. I'll get it now.

ARKASHA. Off you go then.

SLAVIK. Right. (*He turns to go and then stops.*) What about tomorrow?

ARKASHA. Why are you being so difficult, Slavik? You taking me for a ride? Two can play at that, eh . . . You just mucking me round? If you haven't got one, then just come right out and say it.

SLAVIK. Alright. I'll go and get it. (*He runs off.*)

LERA *jumps off the scales.*

ARKASHA. How much beef on you, then?

LERA. Not much.

ARKASHA. Emaciation, they call that.

LERA. Enough. I'm about right.

ARKASHA. A hundred?

LERA (*laughing*). Less than that. Fifty-two.

ARKASHA. Right and how much is beef at the moment? About forty. (*Taps on his calculator.*) So that's about two thousand. I'll buy some for a kebab.

LERA. Go ahead.

ARKASHA. And what if I do.

LERA *laughs.*

I'm joking, aren't I.

LERA. Hey, guess what? I won twelve thousand dollars today!

ARKASHA. Well, how about that. Well done.

LERA. Yeah. It's this Moscow firm called Euroshop and they have these three prizes. One for twenty-five thousand, one for seven-and-a-half and I've won twelve.

ARKASHA. Amazing.

LERA. Yeah. They've got their office at the main post office. It's all official and that. I've got my own registration number and I got this envelope . . . opened it and it said I'd got a prize. I almost dropped dead when I saw it.Yul'ka here saw me. I just stood there, couldn't believe my eyes. Twelve thousand all for me. The envelope was like one of those magazines – all different pictures and that. The stuff they sell. And my name was printed on the front. I've never seen my name in print before. Put me in a spin.

ARKASHA. Well, congratulations, eh.

LERA. And there was this photo of an old woman – like one of those peasant farmworkers. More peasant than

me. She's holding money, a whole load. On a tray.
She's the one who won before me. Last month or
whatever. So I'll be in a photo too. Can you see that?

ARKASHA (*nodding*). I can.

LERA. I'd put some make-up on and do my hair in
curlers, or even go and have a perm. But she was just
some ordinary plain old cow. I'm going to buy myself
a flat straightaway. A car. What sort of car have you
got?

ARKASHA. I've got two cars.

LERA. And is one of those pick-ups a good car?

ARKASHA. Past it.

LERA. Well, I fancy one of those anyway. I'll need to
carry round my goods. 'Cause that's the other thing I
want. I'm going to get a shop. And a pick-up's the
best thing for that. And then maybe I'll buy a Lada
a bit later. In bridal white. I'll be all in my fur jacket
climbing out of a Lada . . . with an alarm and fur
seats . . . music and all . . . Wow! Beep-beep! (*She
turns an imaginary wheel and drives around the room,
making car noises.*)

ARKASHA *laughs.* YUL'KA *smiles.*

The only thing is I've got a problem.

ARKASHA. No curlers?

LERA. No, it's not that. It's . . . Well, how can I put it . . .
It's that . . . I dunno . . . There's this thing, see . . .
how can I say . . . Well, I need to put in an order. Like,
I've got to become their customer and that. 'Cause
they've only got the right to give me the prize then.
Like, legally . . .

ARKASHA. Ahhh.

LERA. And just at the moment . . . See, well, it's all
turned out really badly. I've just had my kitchen
redone. And it was expensive stuff we had. Real
nightmare. But very contemporary. A dishwasher and
all, if you see what I mean.

ARKASHA *nods.*

And I've got no money at all. Like, bad timing . . .

ARKASHA. Aahhh.

LERA. So, I was wondering if you could . . . God, this is
so hard . . .

ARKASHA. Hard like pissing in a postbox, eh . . .

LERA. I was wondering if you could, perhaps lend us
something . . . ?

ARKASHA. Sure.

LERA. Only a thousand roubles.

ARKASHA. Sure.

LERA. And I'll give you two back.

ARKASHA. Sure.

LERA. What, really?

ARKASHA. Sure.

LERA. Shit, you've really helped me. I've been round
everyone's today. And everyone's skint. I was at the
end of my tether. All that money disappearing . . .

SLAVIK *enters, dragging a grave-marker.*

ARKASHA. Well, look who it isn't. So what about all
this 'tomorrow, tomorrow' stuff.

LERA. So you really will give it to me?

ARKASHA. Yeah, yeah.

LERA. Yul'ka, bloody hell! Fantastic! The fur coat, the white Lada, the works! Wow! (*She hugs* YUL'KA.)

ARKASHA. What about the photo, Slavik? You know . . .

SLAVIK. Arkan, I just haven't managed . . .

ARKASHA. Get it off now.

SLAVIK. Won't take me a second. (*He grabs the screwdriver and begins unscrewing the photograph.*)

DIMA *appears.*

DIMA. Where did that one come from?

ARKASHA. Slavik brought it round from his.

DIMA. You cunning bastard, Slav. You said there wasn't any more.

ARKASHA. Not a Jew, are you, Slav?

SLAVIK. No.

DIMA. Yeah, he's a Jew most likely. Hey, Arkash, once he hid five hundred from me in his sock.

ARKASHA. Slava's a Jew! Slava's a Jew (*Roars with laughter.*) Let's have him circumcised!

Everyone laughs. SLAVIK *keeps on unscrewing the photograph.*

DIMA. What are you making such heavy weather of it for? Give it here.

SLAVIK. I'll do it.

DIMA. Give it here. (*He takes the screwdriver from him and pushes him away.*)

SLAVIK *moves back.* DIMA *starts unscrewing the photograph.*

LERA. Dima, guess what, Arkady here . . . (*To* ARKASHA.) You're name's Arkady, right?

ARKASHA. Nah. Just Arkash.

LERA. Hey, guess what, Dim. Arkady's giving me a thousand. Not like you.

DIMA. What, really?

LERA. Yeah.

DIMA. Well then, look pleased about it.

LERA (*offended*). I am.

ARKASHA. So why aren't you dancing?

Pause.

LERA. Do I have to?

ARKASHA. What did you think?

LERA. Well, I . . .

ARKASHA. Striptease, eh, Dima?

DIMA. That's it.

LERA. Well, I . . .

ARKASHA. Come on, we were just having you on. Weren't we, Dima?

DIMA. No.

LERA. You can piss off.

DIMA (*unscrewing a screw and pulling the photograph loose*). Come on, you bugger . . . that's it . . . there we are . . .

The second screw breaks and the photograph breaks away from the marker. DIMA looks at it and suddenly his expression changes completely. He opens his mouth and looks across at SLAVIK. SLAVIK is backing towards the door.

LERA. What?

DIMA. I . . . I . . .

He takes a step in SLAVIK's *direction.* SLAVIK *runs out onto the landing, slams the door and holds it shut with his back, his legs pressed against the stair rails. He does his muppet impression.* DIMA *runs after him and throws himself against the door, shouting. Everyone follows him.* DIMA *kicks the door and stabs it with the screwdriver. The splinters fly off.*

I'll kill you, you bastard! I'll kill you! You'll wish you were dead! I warned you! Open the door! I'll kill you! Open up! Open the door! (*Shrieks.*)

ARKASHA. What's wrong, Dim? Are you ill?

DIMA (*looking at* ARKASHA *with a mad expression*). Fuck off!

ARKASHA. What?!

DIMA. Fuck off! Or I'll have your eye out! (*He advances towards* ARKASHA.)

ARKASHA. Eh . . . Watch it . . . (*He rushes back into the room.*)

DIMA. And you lot, you cunts! Get out of my sight!

YUL'KA *and* LERA *go back into the room.* DIMA *walks about the hall from side to side, declaiming:*

Cunts! The whole lot of them! (*He shrieks, cries, throws himself at the door and falls down.*) Open the door! Open it! I said open it!

He gets up and goes into the room, where ARKASHA *is twisting his finger at his temple to indicate madness.* ARKASHA *and* LERA *make their way towards the balcony.* DIMA *looks at them indifferently. He runs around the room as if searching for something. He can't find it. He goes over to the grave-marker which*

SLAVIK *brought and kneels by it. He picks up the photograph and lifts it to his face.*

Bastard . . . bastard . . .

LERA. What's going on, Dima?

DIMA. Mum, why? Why? Mum . . . why? What's the point of it all? What are we all living for, eh? You brought me into life and I'm nothing, Mum . . . I'm like the walking dead, Mum. I'm dead like you . . . yeah, dead . . . Mum. I don't exist . . . I don't exist!! I don't exist . . .

ARKASHA. Stop that, Dima.

LERA. He's right. Why don't we have a nice drink . . .

DIMA *doesn't answer, but carries on whispering 'I don't exist.'* ARKASHA, LERA *and* YUL'KA *stand motionless, afraid to move.* THE WASTER *sits up in his bed and listens. He cries quietly as if he understands everything.* SLAVIK *unpeels himself from the door and walks down the stairs on stiff stilt-like legs. As he goes he does his muppet impression. He gets to the third floor and then suddenly for some reason he returns. He knocks quietly at the door of the flat under* DIMA*'s with his long bony fingers. Then takes a run at the door and kicks it on the lock with his long stilt-like leg. The door flies open.* SLAVIK *goes into the darkness of the room where the* OLD WOMAN *is lying helpless on the metal bed. He gropes around in the bed. The* OLD WOMAN *wakes up.*

OLD WOMAN. I'm thirsty, Kolya.

SLAVIK. Me too, Mum.

OLD WOMAN. Bring me some water, Kolya.

SLAVIK. Give me a hundred.

OLD WOMAN. I haven't got it, Kolya.

SLAVIK. You've got lots, Mum.

OLD WOMAN. I haven't got it.

SLAVIK. You won't give me any then.

OLD WOMAN. Water, Kolya . . .

SLAVIK. You won't give me any then.

OLD WOMAN. Water, Kolya . . .

SLAVIK. You won't give me any then. (*He lifts a heavy stool above his head.*)

OLD WOMAN. Water, Kolya . . .

SLAVIK. You won't give me any then.

OLD WOMAN. Water, Kolya . . .

SLAVIK. Have a drink then . . . (*He hits her.*)

> DIMA *shudders. He looks at his hands. A ladybird is sitting on one of his palms.* DIMA *sees it and smiles.*

DIMA. Look, a ladybird!

LERA. It's a firefly. From the cemetery. There's lots of them there.

DIMA. You don't know anything. It's a ladybird. Four years old. Four dots. Look . . . Ladybird ladybird, fly away home. Your house is on fire, your children are gone . . .

> *The ladybird crawls across his palm and right to the very tip of his index finger, lifts the orange wings covered in black dots like pieces of earth, straightens them and flies. It circles the room and then flies out of the open balcony door. Into the dark, the night.*

Told you so . . . told you so . . .

He runs out onto the balcony and looks into the autumnal night sky following the ladybird with his eyes, as if he could see it. He smiles.

SLAVIK *finds an ant in the old lady's bed and licks it up, frowning.*

THE WASTER *gets down under the blanket and rolls himself into a tiny ball. He shakes all over with the cold. The wind chases the grey, dead leaves on the road, slams the doors, wails and howls in the entrance halls. People go over to their windows and look out. They are waiting for something.* ARKASHA *twists his finger at his temple.*

Darkness.

End of Act One.

ACT TWO

*It is night. The lights are no longer shining at windows.
Everyone is asleep. A tall dark shadow stands in a
puddle on the street. He is looking at the reflection of the
half-moon beneath his feet. He bends over and touches
the reflection with one hand. The reflection shimmers, is
broken up. The* MAN *squats down and plays with the
reflection. He seems to be laughing. And then he lies down
in the puddle and embraces it, pours it over himself . . .*

In the main room of DIMA's *flat stand three grave-
markers as if in a cemetery. The little iron wreaths on
them are old and blackened, little bunches of lilies. There
are even mixed sweets in front of them.* DIMA *is sitting
on the floor in the corner and looking at his installation.
Admiring it. He is already very drunk.* ARKASHA *and*
LERA *are in the armchair,* LERA *sitting happily on*
ARKASHA's *lap, smoking his cigarettes.* YUL'KA *is
out on the balcony.*

LERA. Like a bloody cemetery it is in here. Dima, get
rid of all this stuff.

DIMA *doesn't answer.*

ARKASHA. And you, Miss Fifty-Two Kilos, down you
get now.

LERA. Don't want to. I've found myself a lovely man.
Anyone would kill for this. My luck's in – got myself
money and a man all at once. There is a God after all.

DIMA. No there isn't.

LERA. Cock off, eh.

ARKASHA. Come on. Get off now.

LERA. No way. Tell me you'll marry me, then I will.

ARKASHA. Sure.

LERA. And why not? I'm a rich bride now, with a flat and a shop. And even a fur coat. The whole set-up. So . . .

ARKASHA. Get off then, rich bride.

LERA. So will you marry me?

ARKASHA. Sure.

LERA. We'll have a family business. I'll give you loads of kids. You'll need to get a moustache, that's the only thing. I've always dreamed of a man with a moustache. Straightaway it looks important, like a professor or something. Will you grow one?

ARKASHA. Sure.

LERA (*touching him on his upper lip*). It would suit you, too. (*She holds a lock of her hair against his lip,*) Wow! Sexy! Want to look in a mirror?

ARKASHA. Later. Get down . . .

LERA. Kiss first.

ARKASHA. After the wedding.

LERA. On the cheek then.

ARKASHA. Hardly worth the effort on the cheek. (*He pushes* LERA.) Get down.

LERA *reluctantly moves into the other armchair.* ARKASHA *stretches his legs.*

LERA. See, Dima. There you go. I've been taken in. I'm going to get married. And you said no-one would have me. Someone has, see. God helped me. If you have faith then God helps. (*To* ARKASHA.) Shit, I've

become really religious recently. When I see a black
cat run across my path, that's it. I can't go on. I can
stand there for up to an hour. If anyone takes out the
rubbish, I run so as to pass them when they've got a
full bucket, 'cause it's bad luck to catch them with an
empty one. And, right, it's all true, actually. Like,
when the cemetery used to work, there were funerals
all the time, and if you walk into a funeral procession
it's bad luck. So everyone went round having bad
luck. Now they've closed it and that's it. Straightaway
I feel happier than ever before. And they're taking
Dima in the army.

ARKASHA. Well, that's a stroke of good luck . . .

DIMA. I'm going to ask to go to Chechnya.

LERA. Cock off – what you going to do there?

ARKASHA. Do you know how much they pay there?

LERA. If they kill you, you're not going to need it.

DIMA. I'm not going for the money.

LERA. They'll still kill you.

DIMA. Well, so what? I might manage to take someone
with me . . .

LERA. You're like a little baby, Dima. Why you going to
kill them? What did they ever do to you?

DIMA. 'S the way it is.

LERA. You can cock off with your ''S the way it is' –
no-one just does that for no reason.

ARKASHA. So what would be a good reason?

LERA. Nothing. I reckon, see, that if I was God, I would
do it like this . . . if I knew that someone was trying
to do something nasty to someone else . . . like kill
them or nick something off them . . . I would get that

person . . . the one who wanted to do the bad deed . . . and paralyse them so they couldn't do it . . . Only for a while . . .

ARKASHA. Well, you're stupid. I would do the opposite. If I wanted someone to die, I'd think about it and they'd go and die . . . Yeah, Dima? You could invent Slavik some terrible death . . . Like he'd be so off his head that he'd get tired walking down the road and lie down for a rest and the next morning there'd be a frost, eh, Dim?

DIMA. There'd be no people left.

ARKASHA *thinks for a second and then roars with laughter.*

ARKASHA. You're not wrong! We'd have all bashed our fucking brains out long ago . . .

He laughs.

LERA (*shouts out to the balcony*). Come and sit with us, Yul'ka!

YUL'KA. I want to stay out here.

LERA. She's in a strop for some reason. I'll go and get her.

She goes out to the balcony.

ARKASHA (*whispering*). Dima, is she . . . offering her services or something?

DIMA. Dunno.

ARKASHA. 'Cause like it seems as if she is. I mean, she's quite forward and that – already asked for money, wants me to give her a thousand.

DIMA. Well, give it to her then.

ARKASHA. Are you having a laugh? If I gave in to all of them, the bed would break. Although she's not the worst I've seen. I could go for it. I'd pay if she was offering. Not a thousand, of course. More like a hundred. Could you let her know? Make a hint?

DIMA. You want it. You let her know.

ARKASHA. Dima, I've done so much for you . . .

DIMA. You want it. You let her know.

ARKASHA. Well, don't go asking me for anything.

He takes the packet of crisps and eats.

On the balcony:

LERA. Hey, guess what, Yul'ka. Arkasha's been saying about getting married to me. Eh?

YUL'KA. Congratulations.

LERA. Bit early for that. I'm still thinking. Till morning. I was just starting to get off with him and then I remembered this rotten tooth I've got. Got to go and get it seen to. Bet it stinks. How embarrassing. What a total fucking mess. Hey . . . (*She breathes on YUL'KA.*) How's that?

YUL'KA. Fine.

LERA. Like hell it is. I can tell. (*She breathes on her hand and sniffs it.*) Never mind. When I get this money, I'll have a posh filling and bridges made of platinum or whatever. Nice, eh? Do you reckon he's after my money?

YUL'KA. I don't know.

Pause.

LERA. Well, who cares. Even if he is. Everything costs now. Marriages of convenience are sometimes even the strongest ones. That's what they say. Psychologists . . . Some of them say that . . . I'm not like head-over-heels about him yet, either. I mean, I like him and all that. You should see him in a moustache! Really suited him! I did him one like this. (*Shows* YUL'KA.) It was – wow! He promised to grow one. He's going to do everything for me, anything I fancy. Did you see when I asked him for money? D'you reckon anyone else would have given it to me? They'd have told me where to go. But he fancied me from the first or something. He stayed, didn't he? Didn't go. 'Cause of me, 'course. No, he's not after my money. He's a . . . you know . . . works with metals. He's got two cars for starters. But he's a criminal. As soon as we get married all that will be over. We'll open a kiosk or a shop. The future is in small and medium-sized businesses. They said that on the TV. He'll go and fetch the goods and I'll sit there and sell them. There's only one problem. All these wholesale markets are run by women. He'll be off with them before you can say it. I'll have to go with him. And find a salesgirl for the shop. It's all trouble with these men, isn't it? Come in, have a drink.

YUL'KA. Don't want to.

LERA. What you being like that for?

YUL'KA. Like what?

LERA. Moping around.

YUL'KA. It's nothing.

LERA. Hey, come on, you, you're my favourite cousin. We'll take you into the business. Fancy it?

YUL'KA. Let's see.

LERA. You'll be all in furs, the works.

YUL'KA. Let's see.

LERA. What's bitten you?

YUL'KA. Nothing.

LERA. You're in a mood. I'll send Dima out to you. He'll cheer you up. (*She shouts.*) Dima, come here! Yul'ka's calling you. Dima! (*To* YUL'KA.) I'm going back to mine . . . I'm missing my sweetie-pie already.

She laughs and goes back into the room.

Dima, go on. Yul'ka wants you.

DIMA. What for?

LERA. Go on.

DIMA. She can come in here.

LERA. Leave me alone with my bloke, why don't you.

ARKASHA. Dima . . .

DIMA. Right.

He gets up and goes out to the balcony and stands next to YUL'KA. *They are silent.* LERA *goes over to* ARKASHA. *She wants to get back on his lap.* ARKASHA *stops her.*

LERA. Liked the moustaches . . .

ARKASHA. I've got to head off in a minute.

LERA. Why?

ARKASHA. Business.

LERA. But it's night.

ARKASHA. Night business.

LERA. I'll come with you.

ARKASHA. You can't.

LERA. Why not?

ARKASHA. You can't and that's that.

LERA. Going to see your other women, eh?

ARKASHA. Maybe.

LERA. What about me? Is that it then?

ARKASHA. We have a spiritual relationship. And I wouldn't mind a physical one.

LERA. What do you mean?

ARKASHA. Three guesses. (*He laughs.*)

LERA. And you can't have one with me?

ARKASHA. You don't want to.

LERA. Why not? I do . . .

ARKASHA. Let's go then.

LERA. To yours?

ARKASHA. The other room.

LERA. The waster's in there.

ARKASHA. The kitchen, then.

LERA. The kitchen?

ARKASHA. And?

LERA. Nothing. Let's go . . .

ARKASHA. Come on then.

LERA. Only, say again that you'll marry me first.

ARKASHA. Sure.

LERA. Really?

ARKASHA. Sure.

LERA. 'Cause I had one bloke who led me a right old dance and then it turned out he was married. Two kids and that. One was a student, the other had it's own kids. A grandad and he was having it that he was thirty. You're not married, at least?

ARKASHA. No.

LERA. And you haven't got any grandchildren?

ARKASHA. Are you nuts? I'm twenty-seven.

LERA. That's what the other guy said.

ARKASHA. Come on. (*He goes into the kitchen.*)

LERA. I'm just coming. You go on in.

> ARKASHA *goes out.* LERA *pours herself some wine
> and drinks. She gargles the wine. Then she breathes in
> her hand and sniffs. She gargles again. Then she
> follows him.* YUL'KA *looks in from the balcony and
> whispers something.*

DIMA. What?

YUL'KA. Nothing. Talking to myself.

DIMA. Are you staying with them?

YUL'KA. No way. I'm just doing a course here. Our
relatives aren't even on speaking terms. Her mum's an
alcoholic and my dad, her brother, yeah, is a dean at
college. I didn't even know she existed. I was sitting in
this big group and we found each other quite by chance.
Then we had a little celebration, and that was it . . .

They are silent.

So this area is called 'Dead and Alive', is it?

DIMA. Just the block. Not the area. A bit further along
are some barracks, maybe you saw them . . . well,
they've half pulled them down. And there's only the
dross living up here. When they built the block, all the
sane ones paid something to move out. 'Cause back
then you couldn't sell the flats – just exchange them
and pay something extra. We used to have a big flat.
You know, the old-fashioned sort.

YUL'KA. Uh-huh.

DIMA. Anyway, the waster exchanged it and drank his way through the difference. And Lera's mum did the same. Depressing, isn't it. There are still some normal people living here. Even still got their own cars . . . well, clapped-out old bangers anyway. The garages are over there. Workers and that. But now you can't even sell a flat up here. It's a shithole. No-one would move here.

YUL'KA. Uh-huh.

DIMA. Anyway, I'm not coming back after the army. There's nothing here. Like they reckon that the cemetery over there's finished – well, we've been living in the cemetery ourselves for a long time. We're the living dead. We're born and straightaway we're sent over there. Born and over there. And on the way we nick the grave-markers and drink a tankload of spirits. And that's it. And straight over there. Before, when they weren't taking the metal, we used to bring the sweets back by the bucketful. Made home brew with them. Our neighbour used to make cakes with them. The sweets were the filling. And people used to make chocolate-biscuit cake with the biscuits, and like, stuff like that. Everyone had their own patch, and you didn't dare to try anyone else's. We had big battles with the gypsies. That was crazy . . . the number of people collecting stuff . . . (*He laughs.*) I remember . . . I was going to school and it was my birthday and so I collected up some sweets – like, d'you remember those 'swallow' chocolates, or . . . what's it called, 'storm herald' sweets. I got three for everyone. Usually everyone brought two each, but I had three. Well, they were fuck . . . er, well impressed . . . (*He laughs.*) So I gave them out, all full of myself and they were all sitting there, unwrapping them and then . . . (*He laughs.*) All these ants crawled out. And everyone knew I lived by the cemetery. Nightmare!

You can imagine what followed. Like, they wouldn't let me into the Pioneers until later because of all that. Nightmare, that was. There was this one girl and something happened, you know, mentally to her, 'cause after that either she couldn't eat or she couldn't go to the toilet for a week. Yeah . . . crazy . . . I was on probation with the police for a while after that.

YUL'KA. Very amusing.

DIMA. I tell you, it was that. Only, now I'm laughing but back then I wanted to kill myself. I was so embarrassed. We had this fat guy, Sanya, in our class and he didn't care less. He says, you don't want the sweets, I'll eat them. The teacher took them all off him. Anyway, afterwards, me and him became mates and he used to come round to mine to eat sweets. He ate them, ants and all . . . (*He laughs.*)

YUL'KA. Very amusing. (*She yawns.*)

They are silent.

DIMA. I've got to go round to my mum's grave later and put everything back in its place. It's dark now and I'll have trouble finding it, but I might not manage it later. I have to be at the recruiting office by six. Will you help? 'Cause that lot will probably leave, I expect.

YUL'KA. Alright. Only, I'm afraid of dead people.

DIMA. What for? It's the live ones you need to watch . . .

YUL'KA. Well, I won't get scared if I'm with you.

DIMA. Nor me with you.

YUL'KA. No – I'm a complete coward though. You aren't. I really liked it when you wanted to take that bloke's eye out. He completely gave in. Is he mafia or something?

DIMA. I can't remember. I lost it a bit.

YUL'KA. Yeah, you did well. Good man. That's how to treat them.

DIMA. Let's forget about it, eh.

YUL'KA. Could you have done it?

DIMA. What?

YUL'KA. Taken his eye out with the screwdriver.

DIMA. Dunno.

YUL'KA. Or killed him?

DIMA. No.

YUL'KA. But what about over me?

DIMA. Dunno.

YUL'KA. Like, for example, if he did something bad to me . . .

DIMA. Depends what.

YUL'KA. Well, like, if he raped me.

DIMA. I might kill him.

YUL'KA. How?

DIMA. A knife . . . through the heart.

YUL'KA. Or the throat?

DIMA. Dunno. I could . . .

YUL'KA (*her voice shaking*). Only for me, though, yeah? Say it.

DIMA. Yeah.

They are silent.

YUL'KA. Dima . . .

DIMA. What?

YUL'KA. I really like it that you'd do anything for me.
You wouldn't do that for just anyone, would you?

DIMA. No.

YUL'KA. You wouldn't for Lera?

DIMA. Dunno.

YUL'KA. Say you wouldn't.

DIMA. I wouldn't.

YUL'KA. I know that. I just wanted to hear it from you.
Just for me, then?

DIMA. Yeah.

YUL'KA. Yes?

DIMA. Yes.

YUL'KA. YES?!

DIMA. Yes.

> YUL'KA *suddenly grabs his head and takes his lower
> lip in her teeth. She bites him and wraps her leg
> around him like a snake. Then, just as suddenly, she
> moves away, breathing heavily.* DIMA *makes a
> movement in her direction.*

YUL'KA. That's enough!

DIMA. Why?

YUL'KA. I said, that's enough. Later . . .

> *They are silent for a long time. They smoke.*

> Dima . . .

DIMA. What?

YUL'KA. Dima, they've been telling me that Lera, like,
you know, hangs around the station . . . like, goes
with men . . . for twenty roubles and that. Like . . .
a prostitute. Is it true?

DIMA. I don't know.

YUL'KA. Don't give me that, Dima. I'm just asking. I'm not going to tell her.

DIMA. I don't know.

YUL'KA. Oh come on, Dim . . . What you being like that for? I'm going to write to you. Make an effort . . .

DIMA. Well, maybe . . . I mean, something like that might of . . . didn't see it myself . . .

YUL'KA. What, for twenty roubles?

DIMA. Dunno. Maybe.

YUL'KA. Why so cheap?

DIMA. Dunno.

YUL'KA. Well, I suppose she isn't worth much more, is she?

DIMA. Dunno.

YUL'KA. So why was she getting so worked up about that bloke her mum brought round then?

DIMA. How should I know?

YUL'KA. Like, making herself out to be a fresh little virgin, all 'butter wouldn't melt' and that – when she's a twenty-rouble slag . . . eh?

DIMA. Let's not talk about it . . . it's her problem.

YUL'KA. And what sort of a slag am I?

DIMA. You're not a slag.

YUL'KA. Well, how much would you pay for me? Would you give a million?

DIMA. No.

YUL'KA. Two?

DIMA. None. You're not a slag.

YUL'KA. True. I'm beautiful, aren't I, Dim?

DIMA. What?

YUL'KA. You fancy me, don't you . . .

DIMA. Well, yeah . . . s'pose . . .

YUL'KA. I know. 'Cause everyone fancies me. I'm a D-cup.

DIMA. What? Your legs or something?

YUL'KA. Stupid. Up here. (*She touches her breasts.*) Peaches, they are. Lera's are all droopy already. Like spaniel's ears. You don't fancy her, do you? She's ugly, isn't she?

DIMA. I don't know much about that.

YUL'KA. Say you don't fancy her, or I won't write to you.

DIMA. I don't. Happy?

YUL'KA. There you are then. And I've got a tattoo, as well.

DIMA. A what?

YUL'KA. A tattoo, idiot. Right on my arse. A panther. Want to have a look?

DIMA. What?

YUL'KA. You do . . . you do . . . you do . . .

DIMA. I do.

YUL'KA. Well, talk about sly. First kiss my hand.

She stretches out her hand. DIMA *kisses it.*

Now every finger. That's it. I'm the most beautiful, aren't I?

DIMA. Yes.

YUL'KA. More beautiful than Madonna?

DIMA. Yes.

YUL'KA. And Sharon Stone?

DIMA. More beautiful.

YUL'KA. That's it then. The most beautiful . . .

DIMA. Yes.

YUL'KA. Of everyone . . .

DIMA. Yes.

YUL'KA. Would you jump off the balcony for me?

DIMA. What?

YUL'KA. Could you jump off the balcony for me?

DIMA. What for?

YUL'KA. For me.

DIMA. Why?

YUL'KA. 'Cause I want you to. 'Cause I'm a vamp,
I am . . . Lady Fate, that's me . . . Could you? One
guy cut his veins 'cause of me. With a razor right here.
(*She demonstrates.*) Here and here and the whole bath
was filled with blood. All red. And him as white as a
snowflake. White all over . . . (*She laughs.*) And his
mother came round and said to me, 'You little cunt.
He did that because of you.' And I told her that it was
because of me, but I'm no cunt. And she wanted to
fight me. Well, I lost interest then. Everyone was really
jealous of me. And he was white as snow. I only kissed
him the once and that was it. He wasn't attractive. All
skinny. Stupid prick. Yuk! So anyway – have you lost
your nerve?

DIMA. No.

YUL'KA. Jump then.

DIMA. I thought you were –

YUL'KA. Don't think – just jump.

DIMA. Why do you need this?

YUL'KA. Idiot. You don't understand. You've wimped out.

DIMA. I haven't.

YUL'KA. Jump then.

DIMA (*calmly*). I will then.

YUL'KA. Go on then. Look at me! (*She lifts her top.*) Yeah! Look! You daft prick! You won't see any more like this . . . Jump!

DIMA *climbs onto the railing.*

Go on then!

DIMA *stands up straight and holds onto the washing lines.*

Let go!

DIMA *lets go and balances.*

Jump, stupid!

DIMA. Show me your tattoo!

YUL'KA. Jump first! Jump! Jump!

DIMA *leans backwards.* LERA *runs onto the balcony. She grabs* YUL'KA *by the hair and bangs her down on her knee.* YUL'KA *tears free and runs back into the room laughing hysterically. She hides behind* ARKASHA. LERA *drags* DIMA *off the railings and goes back into the room.* DIMA *sits down on the ground.*

LERA. What the fuck d'you think you're doing?

YUL'KA. What's it to do with you, you twenty-rouble slag!

LERA. What did you say?!

YUL'KA. Twenty-rouble slag! I know all about you! Railway station tart! (*To* ARKASHA.) Did you know she was a prostitute down at the station?

ARKASHA. Eh-eh.

LERA. What are you going on about? Cock off! What do you mean, prostitute . . . ? I'm not –

ARKASHA. I don't under –

YUL'KA. Goes with tramps.

ARKASHA. Eh-eh. Now you're in trouble . . .

LERA. She's making it up!

ARKASHA. Come here!

YUL'KA. She's got syphilis!

ARKASHA. Eh-eh . . .

LERA. What are you on about, you bitch? I'll kill you! She's lying . . .

ARKASHA. I said come here!

LERA *moves away.*

If I bloody well catch something, you'll be dead meat. Come here!

LERA *sits in the corner and covers her face with her hands.*

YUL'KA. Punch her face in!

ARKASHA *goes over to* LERA.

LERA (*indifferently*). Just not on my head. I can't –

ARKASHA. Why didn't you warn me?

LERA. I haven't got anything.

ARKASHA. You'd better be right.

LERA. I know.

ARKASHA. Are you sure?

LERA. Yes.

ARKASHA. You watch out, eh . . . I'll get you, eh . . . and I'll bury you . . .

Kicking LERA *in the stomach.* LERA *doesn't react.*

Didn't that hurt, eh?

YUL'KA. Punch her face!

ARKASHA. Shall I, eh?

LERA. Just not on my head . . .

ARKASHA. And why not?

He kicks her again. LERA *doesn't react.* YUL'KA *roars with laughter.*

Let's try it, eh!

LERA. Just not on my head . . .

ARKASHA *kicks her even harder.* LERA *quietly cries out.*

ARKASHA. That one got through, did it? Again?

LERA *doesn't answer.*

YUL'KA. No answer means yes.

ARKASHA. Again?

LERA *is silent.*

Alright, that's enough, bitch. (*To* YUL'KA.) I'm going now. Coming with me? Didn't you say you were from the town?

YUL'KA. Let's finish their drink first.

Pause.

ARKASHA. Well . . . alright then. There's no police around early morning, anyway. (*He sits down and pours a drink.*)

YUL'KA. You men are so weird. Always throwing yourselves at right dogs. It's not like there aren't any normal women . . .

ARKASHA. Yeah, but you were all wrapped up in yourself.

YUL'KA. I was watching. It was fun – scenes from the everyday life of a prostitute. (*Laughs.*)

LERA. I didn't expect anything like this from you, cousin. I –

YUL'KA. I'm no cousin of yours. You reckon you've found yourself a cousin – I wouldn't hang round you if you were the last person alive. I mean, cousins . . . (*She roars with laughter.*) My dad is almost sick if you mention her mum's name.

ARKASHA. Dross, are they?

YUL'KA. 'Course they are! That outfit she's in is her only one! She wears it everyday.

LERA. Well, it's not my fault if my mum drinks all the –

ARKASHA. So why was she going on to me about re-doing the kitchen?

YUL'KA. She was having you on. You're a bit naïve.

ARKASHA. So it seems.

LERA (*to* ARKASHA). You promised me money.

ARKASHA. Dima owes me a twenty. You can take it off him. (*He laughs.*)

LERA. You promised a thousand!

ARKASHA (*laughing*). She's got a bloody nerve!

LERA. So you won't give it to me?

ARKASHA. I never meant to anyway.

LERA. I'll give you back two . . . or even three.

YUL'KA. Where from?

LERA. You know where from. When I get the –

YUL'KA. When you get what? You're not getting anything! (*Laughing, to* ARKASHA.) Guess what she thinks? She got this letter from some 'Euroshop' – like, you know, prizes and all that. Total rip-off stuff.

LERA. Don't lie . . .

YUL'KA. Like, one of those 'you have already won a prize, but in order to participate in our lottery you need to make a purchase' – for gullible idiots.

LERA. Don't lie . . .

YUL'KA. So there's about a hundred thousand prize-winning idiots . . .

LERA. Don't lie . . .

YUL'KA. I'm not . . . My mum ordered once from one of those firms. She got some crappy camera. The rubbishy ones. It doesn't even take pictures . . .

LERA. Don't lie . . .

ARKASHA. Yeah! I've got one of those at home! Now I remember. I was wondering what she was going on about . . . dollars and that . . . Hasn't even got a flash, has it?

YUL'KA. Yeah, you have to buy the flash seperately . . . Crap, it is . . . rubbish.

LERA. Don't lie. (*She is on the verge of crying.*)

YUL'KA. Pointless explaining it to you – your brains are half-eaten away with the syphilis . . .

ARKASHA. That's enough of that.

YUL'KA. Too late for scaring you. Pour me a drink.

ARKASHA *pours a drink.* DIMA *comes in from the balcony.*

ARKASHA. Hey, Dima, I've got a bone to pick . . . You never told me that she –

DIMA (*calmly*). Right. Get the fuck out of here. Both of you.

ARKASHA. What?

DIMA. I said, move it.

YUL'KA *laughs loudly, drinks.*

ARKASHA. Dim, you're taking a few liberties, aren't you . . .

DIMA. You got eyes to spare, have you. (*Picks up the screwdriver.*)

ARKASHA *gets up.*

(*To* YUL'KA.) You and all.

YUL'KA. What did I do to you then?

DIMA. Go on.

YUL'KA *gets up.*

ARKASHA. By the way Dim, you only gave me two grave-markers and I brought stuff to the value of four . . . so part of this is –

DIMA. Take it.

ARKASHA *quickly puts the food in a bag.* YUL'KA *laughs at him.*

That it?

ARKASHA. That's it. You can be thankful you're off to the army or I'd have sent the boys round.

DIMA. Out.

ARKASHA and YUL'KA go to the door. YUL'KA deliberately drops a glass of wine. The glass breaks.

YUL'KA. Accident!

She laughs. DIMA doesn't react. They go out of the flat. DIMA starts picking up the splinters of glass. The sound of loud laughter can be heard, first of all from the landing and then from outside. Then a car starts up and the horn plays the 'Spartak Champion' tune for a while. There is a screech of tyres and the reflection of a light passes across the ceiling. Silence. DIMA puts the splinters on the table and sits down.

They are silent.

LERA. Shouldn't have let her go. Her mum'll bloody kill me . . .

DIMA doesn't answer.

She's really strict, see . . .

DIMA. I have to go. To mum's first of all. To put everything back. Will you help?

LERA. Yes.

Pause.

DIMA. Or just sell it. You need the money. And someone'll take it sooner or later anyway. And when you get the money you can put up some marble thing. They don't get nicked as often . . .

LERA. Forget it, Dim. I'll find the money. You can't do that.

DIMA. Where are you going to find the money? If we leave it, it's just money for booze and at least this way it's some use. At least one person gets helped. Do you know where to take it?

LERA. Yeah.

DIMA. Well, there you go. You sell it and you'll have enough. You can make your order . . .

LERA (*suddenly bursts into tears*). Dima, as soon as I get my money, I'll order a marble one. It's the first thing I'll do. And we'll put it up when you get back on leave.

DIMA. We'll do that . . .

They are silent.

LERA. Write back home. And I'll come round and ask after you . . . because I might move soon . . . buy a flat and that . . .

DIMA. Alright.

LERA. And don't think of not coming back. Who's going to help me? I'm going to have my own business.

DIMA. We'll write to each other . . .

LERA. Yeah, that's what's going to happen . . . once I set my mind on something . . . (*She cries again.*)

DIMA. That's it.

LERA. It is.

DIMA. We'll have everything.

LERA. We will.

They are silent.

DIMA. What's the time?

LERA. I don't know.

DIMA. Time to go, I expect.

LERA. Already?

DIMA. I'm probably late . . . I've still got the whole town to cross . . .

LERA. Let's go then.

DIMA. Let's go.

They get up and put on their coats.

I'll just tell the waster that this is yours so he gives it to you later . . .

LERA. Go on.

DIMA. Hang on.

He goes into THE WASTER*'s room.*

Wast . . . Dad . . .

THE WASTER *doesn't answer.* DIMA *touches his head and then moves away.*

Dad, I'm going. That's it. It's time to go. There are some . . . graves out here . . . they're Lera's . . . Give them to her later, alright? Alright? Well, that's it then. I'm off. Write to me, eh? Alright then . . .

He comes back out.

LERA. Did you tell him?

DIMA. Yeah . . . Let's go . . .

LERA. Let's go.

They go out onto the landing and push the door to. Then they go downstairs silently, trying not to tread on the dry leaves. They go outside and stop, look up at the block with its black eyes for windows. Everyone is still sleeping. Or dead. It isn't clear.

DIMA. We could take a taxi.

LERA. OK.

Pause.

TOGETHER. Cock off. There's no money . . .

They laugh and then suddenly they both start to cry, loudly and without hiding it from each other. They squat and hug each other. Press closer together and cry.

LERA. What's that? (*She points at his face.*)

DIMA. Where?

LERA. On your cheek.

DIMA *runs his hand over his cheek and then looks at his palm.*

Ladybird.

DIMA. The same one.

LERA. Cock off . . .

DIMA. No, look. Four dots. Four years old. It's come back.

LERA. It's a sign.

DIMA. Y'what?

LERA. Nothing.

TOGETHER. Ladybird ladybird, fly away home. Your house is on fire and your children are gone . . .

The ladybird straightens its wings and flies off, minding neither the wind, nor the cold, nor anything else.

DIMA. Let's run after it . . .

LERA. The recruiting office is the other way . . .

DIMA. We'll make it . . . Come on!

They run after the ladybird, both laughing and crying, and are hidden from view. The street is empty. The first window lights up in the block by the cemetery. Someone goes over to the window and looks out, stands there for a minute and then disappears back . . . Into the block.

The first strips of light appear in the east, as red as blood. The first snowflake falls and then another and another. Snow starts falling in earnest. Not a winter snowfall, but a thick, warm one. The whole area, all the dirt, everything is covered in snow. And things seem much brighter somehow. And then it is very bright. Perhaps as it should be.

The End.

A Nick Hern Book

Ladybird first published in Great Britain as a paperback original in
2004 by Nick Hern Books Limited, 14 Larden Road, London W3 7ST
in association with the Royal Court Theatre, London

Cover Image: Luc Delahaye / Magnum Photos

Typeset by Country Setting, Kingsdown, Kent CT14 8ES
Printed and bound in Great Britain by Bookmarque, Croydon, Surrey

A CIP catalogue record for this book is available from
the British Library

ISBN 1 85459 788 4